Lessons

through

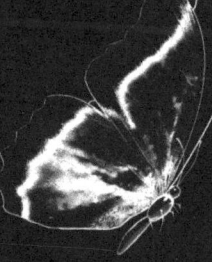

Lyrics

from A to Z

By: Alana Nicole

THIS BOOK
BELONGS TO:

_____

_____

_____

THIS BOOK
IS DEDICATED TO:

To my Momma, LaWanna Faye Rolack. I believe you always knew this day would come—that one day, I'd write a book. Oh, how I wish you were here to see it. I miss you more than words can say. I pray you enjoy it and that I've made you proud. Please keep watching over me and guiding me as I care for my Grands. You were such an amazing grandmother to my children, and I'm doing my best to carry on your beautiful legacy.

I love and miss you deeply. Now go back to dancing, singing, and cracking jokes—just like you always did.

Love you forever and always,
Nicole

Introduction

Welcome to my first written love.

This journey has been a long time coming, and I pray you enjoy it.

This book is my legacy—a blend of my love for music, my passion for educating and helping others, and the life experiences that have shaped me.

I poured my heart into these pages, sharing my testimonies of pain and mistakes, hoping to inspire and support you and others along the way.

So, get comfortable, grab a pen and a snack, and dive in. I hope it resonates with you.

Alana Nicole AKA Mrs. 1 Healthy You

Table of *Contents*

A Song for Mama

It all depends on my mood—LOL! If I'm mad, it's *Party Up* by DMX. Feeling frisky? It might be *Cater to You* by Destiny's Child or *In the Mood* by The Whispers. When I'm deep in my thoughts, it's *Songbird* **by** Kenny G. And if I'm in prayer, it's likely *I Won't Complain* by Rev. Paul Jones or *I Need You* by Shekinah Glory.

Whatever the mood, one thing's for sure: I'll get through the situation, "by hook or by crook," "one way or another," and "sooner or later." And most of the time, a good song helps me along the way.

1 Healthy Y♥u

Hey you!
"Whatchu Like"

What song gets YOU? Embodies YOU? Moves YOU?
What song SPEAKS to you, was MADE just for you,
DESCRIBES you to a T?
What songs do you hear/play/and NEED over and over
again?

_____

_____

_____

_____

_____

_____

_____

_____

_____

_____

_____

Before I Let Go

Ok, I'll be honest. In every major relationship I've been in, I've given chances. When things got bad, we'd take a break, separate, or even break up. This goes for friendships, too. We might stop talking for a while, then come back to revisit the situation or conversation that brought us to that point.

But once I've gained a clear understanding that this just isn't going to work, I let go. Plain and simple. I usually give *two good chances*. First time? Shame on **YOU**. Second time? Shame on **ME**. Third time? Nope! You don't get the opportunity to keep doing **THAT** to me!

At some point in life, you have to choose YOU—for YOU. There comes a time when you must make the difficult decision to let go of what you love, and even what may love you, for the sake of your own growth and well-being.

Let Go*Goals*

Goal 1

(Start Date): _____ (End Date): _____

Action Steps | Notes
○ _____
○ _____
○ _____

Goal 2

(Start Date): _____ (End Date): _____

Action Steps | Notes
○ _____
○ _____
○ _____

Goal 3

(Start Date): _____ (End Date): _____

Action Steps | Notes
○ _____
○ _____
○ _____

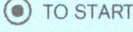 TO START   OK   DELAY 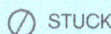 STUCK 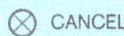 CANCEL

Can You Stand the Rain?

My biggest storm was watching my mom leave me. No one could have ever convinced me it would happen that day, or like that. But it did, and she did—and yet, here we are, still standing. Thank GOD.

I've weathered storms in relationships, life changes, finances, careers, transportation, and credit. Oh yeah, I'm just a regular person with regular problems living a regular life.

I know there are people who almost rejoice when they hear anything negative about me— just to have another reason to dislike me, hold a grudge, turn their nose up, or continue carrying their disdain for me.

AND I MARCH ON.
With my head held high, tears possibly in my eyes, and a sting in my heart, I keep stepping— even in the rainstorm.

When all you can do is stand? Do just that. Brace yourself against something if you have to. Take short breaths. Get through that moment, because this too shall pass.

And when you can't stand? Retreat. Gather yourself. Cry, scream, moan, groan, kick—whatever it takes. Then calm yourself. Pray. Dream. Sit in the quiet and listen to nothing but the air around you. Once you've released it all, begin your plan. Rise. Resurface.

The next day, when yesterday is behind you, give yourself a pat on the back. Because you did that. You fought, you plotted, you planned—and you survived that day's rain.

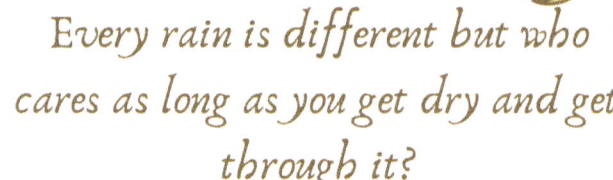

Every rain is different but who cares as long as you get dry and get through it?

Date: ..../..../....

Today, I'm still grateful that I made it through the rain of

_____
_____
_____
_____
_____
_____

The best part of the rain was

_____
_____
_____
_____
_____

Dead and Gone

I'm thankful and grateful for the past I've had, the lessons learned, and the person I'm still evolving into because of it all. I'm happy here. Here feels good and is home.

It straight tickles me to hear my daughters speak of how I used to be. Mannn I didn't realize I looked like a gorilla to them! They say I didn't play! I swear I don't remember the stories the way they do! According to them? I was kicking butts and taking names EVERY day! But God!

Today, I'm much happier and calmer being a better example to them and my Grands. I think before making decisions mostly. And I decide how to handle things in a way best for everyone. At least I try to.

As I got older and saw them watching I had to do things I'd want them to do! If I ain't want them looking crazy I couldn't do so! I had to walk it like I talked it.

Now, I still will not be disrespected, dishonored, used, abused, ignored, manipulated, dogged, lied on, bullied, or belittled. Don't get it twisted. I still have standards; I just defend them differently.

Are you old or new?

Who are you?

_____

_____

What makes you happy?

_____

_____

Where is home?

_____

_____

What does home look/feel like?

_____

_____

Are you the old you or new you? As of when?

_____

_____

End of the Road

Accept life—its changes, challenges, and celebrations—with grace. If you're fortunate enough to live a long life, there will be struggles, and it won't always be perfect. However, how you handle each situation is what determines what happens next.

This applies to everything: the end of a job, a relationship, a friendship, a loss, a birth, a win, or even something as simple as a meal! Think about it—after a meal, are you so stuffed you can barely move? Or do you leave the table feeling content and at ease? The key is, when you first reach your limit, do you stop yourself? Or do you keep going beyond what's comfortable?

Ahh, makes you think, doesn't it? Good! Now consider a win or a promotion. Are you humble, or are you braggadocious? And what about relationships? Are you overly clingy when things are good and irrational when they end?

The goal is to find balance—a happy middle ground for every road you encounter. Strive for harmony in life as best you can, no matter the circumstances. Maybe it's the Libra in me, but I promise you this: balance is beautiful!

BALANCING YOU

HOME / FAMILY	WORK / WEALTH
YOU	
HEALTH	RELATIONSHIPS

F⊙CUS

Believe in YOU and focus on YOU, even when no one else does.
NEVER lose sight of yourself in your own view!

Yes, other people can be part of your focus, but that doesn't mean you should blur yourself out of the picture.
Here's the truth: you cannot keep making lists, plans, or priorities that don't include YOU at the top.

For years, I shopped without adding myself to the list. Bought groceries without considering what I needed. Made plans where I wasn't a priority. Took care of everyone else, ensuring they were good—except me. I even took pictures of everyone but never included myself.

At the time, I thought I was just being a good person: a good mom, wife, and friend.
Now? I see clearly.
NEVER AGAIN will I lose focus of ME.
Put yourself first, always. You deserve it.

REFLECTION

What's your focus?

How can you achieve it and what are the obstacles?

GOOD GOOD

It's important—for you and for those around you—
that you strive to be good! Understand that you are not
in this world alone, and your sanity and well-being
matter.

First, make it a priority to ensure, as best as you can,
that you are doing well on multiple levels:

- Spiritually
- Individually (mentally, emotionally, physically,
  nutritionally, and financially)
- Collectively (in your relationship with your spouse
  or significant other)
- Domestically (with your household and extended
  family members)
- Socially (with friends)
- Community-wise (in your church, neighborhood,
  workplace, and other groups or organizations)

When making decisions, focus on what is truly best for
you and your situation at that time. I never recommend
making decisions based on self-interest or personal gain
alone. For example, I would never base my income,
purchases, or bills on overtime pay—it can disappear
overnight, literally! Whether you work a job, have a
career, or run a business, you should still be cautious
with your finances.

The bottom line: make the best decisions you can, but avoid using people or situations as a deciding factor. You'll only end up stressed or disappointed. The same principle applies to relationships: don't involve yourself with others solely for personal gain or gratification. If you place too much dependence on someone or something, it almost always ends badly.

A wise woman once told me, "Your kids can't be your everything if you expect them to grow up and be self-sufficient. You're raising them to lead productive lives away from you. If your life revolves entirely around them, what will you do when they leave?"

So, prioritize with boundaries—daily. And when you fall short? Try again, using the knowledge you've gained. Remember, the definition of insanity is doing the same thing repeatedly and expecting a different result.

DAILY PROGRESS TRACKER

REMINDER
WHEN PRIORITIZING
PUT YOUR CREATOR 1ST,
YOU 2ND,
AND GO FROM THERE.

GOOD
NOTES/TRACKER

DATE: _____

_____
_____
_____
_____
_____
_____
_____
_____
_____
_____
_____
_____
_____
_____
_____
_____
_____
_____
_____

HELLO

HELLO'S ARE IMPORTANT, YES!

BUT WHAT IF, INSTEAD OF USING IT AS JUST A GREETING FOR OTHERS, YOU TRIED USING IT FOR YOURSELF?

START EACH MORNING WITH A HELLO TO YOURSELF AND YOUR CREATOR.

SAY HELLO TO A BETTER WAY OF HANDLING SITUATIONS AND EMOTIONS.

SAY HELLO TO YOUR NEW LOOK, YOUR FAVORITE OUTFIT, YOUR WEIGHT LOSS, YOUR SELF-CARE ROUTINES, AND YOUR IMPROVED MENTAL STATE.

LET HELLO BE YOUR SALUTE TO GROWTH, PROGRESS, AND THE BEAUTY OF BECOMING THE BEST VERSION OF YOU!

MY DAILY Hello's

I Wanna Dance with Somebody

Born in Metro Detroit, where legendary hits were made, and raised by parents who loved music, it's no wonder I became the music lover I am today. I often hear a word, note, or phrase and instantly think of a song. Music runs through my veins—I LOVE it! I'm also a picture taker, just like my Momma. Music made her "Lose Control," and with three kids, she sure knew how to "Work It" on a budget. Of course, she was always a LADY who knew how to "Get Ur Freak On." She loved her some Missy Elliott, and every time one of her songs comes on, I can't help but giggle.

What's your jam? Your go-to dance, song, memory, or picture? You've got to have them— for yourself and your loved ones. If you don't, now is the time to start!
I'm a ballad and R&B lover, but I'm versatile. Wanna see me laid out? Put on *Change Me* by Tramaine Hawkins or *Yes* by Shekinah Glory. Wanna see me smile? Try *Promise to Love* by Kem, *You* by Jesse Powell, or *Raise the Bar* by Tamar Braxton.
Thinking about my grands? *I Never Knew Love Like This Before* by Stephanie Mills. And for family vibes? It's all about *We Are One, Family Reunion, or Summer Madness!*

My favorite
song/dance/photo/memories are

_____

_____

_____

_____

_____

_____

_____

_____

_____

_____

_____

_____

_____

JOY AND PAIN

Joy and pain—these are interconnected emotional experiences. They can coexist, often showing up at the same time. In life, we experience both. In an ideal world, we'd have more joy than pain. However, pain still exists and often shows up uninvited.

For example, imagine a loved one who has been ill, perhaps even bedbound, for a long time. When they pass on, logic reminds us they are no longer suffering—joy! But at the same time, our heart, memories, and longing ache for their presence, their voice, their smell—pain. In that moment, joy and pain collide, unbidden and unavoidable.

How you handle both is entirely up to you. It's not easy, especially when love is involved or the situation is abrupt. Proceeding with caution is often the best way forward. When I suddenly lost my mother, all I could do was be still and quiet. Mentally, I was consumed by pain and shock, yet I felt joy knowing she was no longer in pain and was now with our King.

Through pain, try to appreciate and be grateful for the joys you've experienced—whether they're in the present or the past. This gratitude will eventually help you navigate through the pain.

JOY AND PAIN JOURNEY

Date: _____

Today I'm grateful for

- _____
- _____
- _____
- _____
- _____

Today's affirmations

- _____
- _____
- _____

3 GOOD things about today

- _____
- _____
- _____

Something I'm proud of today

- _____
- _____
- _____

1 HEALTHY Y♥U

KNOCKING ON HEAVEN'S DOOR

As we grow older, we come to understand that tomorrow is not promised to anyone. Knowing this, we must strive to live each day as happily as possible, with as little regret as we can manage.
This means being reciprocal in love, respect, manners, standards, and kindness.
Let's treat people the way we want to be treated and approach life with positivity, pleasantries, peace, and productivity. When your time comes, can you say your earthly mission was completed, started, or left untapped?
This book is my proof that one of my missions—to write and help others—has been accomplished.

PLANS

GOAL	PURPOSE	STARTED	DONE

Living for the City

FOR MANY IN THE '70S, THIS WAS THEIR ANTHEM—THEIR VOICE, THEIR LIFE, AND THE RAW EXPRESSION OF EMOTION DURING THAT ERA. TODAY, MANY OF US ARE STILL BATTLING OUR OWN VERSIONS OF GRIT IN OUR LIVES AND CITIES. TO ENDURE THE DIFFICULT AND UNCERTAIN TIMES, WE ALL NEED AN ANTHEM—A SONG THAT FUELS OUR STRENGTH, POWER, HOPE, COURAGE, AND ASPIRATIONS.

What's your anthem song(s)?

For happy times:
- _____
- _____
- _____

For sad times:
- _____
- _____
- _____

Struggles:
- _____
- _____
- _____

Depression:
- _____
- _____
- _____

Celebrations:
- _____
- _____
- _____

Overcoming
- _____
- _____
- _____

Moments in Love

As often as you can, create and cherish
moments in love.

Moments with family, friends, and even by yourself.
Make those moments memorable, rooted in love.

Each year, aim to create several unique moments in
love to treasure and enjoy.

Every year, plan for even more. And every year, take
a moment to reflect and count how many you've
accomplished.

I personally use the calendar as a tool to assess my
life—its memories, blessings, happiness, direction,
and areas that may need adjustment.

1 Healthy You

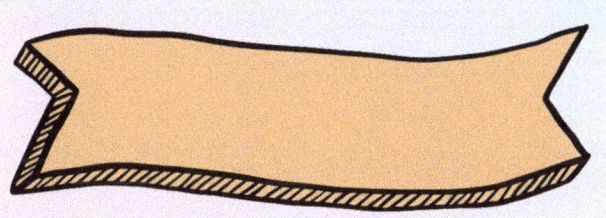

MOMENTS IN LOVE

GOALS	ACTION PLAN	PURPOSE

Never Would Have Made It

I know I can't be the only one with this story!

Oh, just me and Marvin Sapp, huh? You know that's a tale—a bold-faced TALE!

Now, think about it—who got you through that test, interview, selection process, credit check, bad relationship, or health issue? Take any situation you want, and if you're reading this and that chapter is behind you, ask yourself: Who do you think really got you through it?

Ok, little-known fact: I attended a Catholic school for one year. My favorite class? Religion. One of the most profound things I learned was that God works through man or nature.

That means when I got awarded extra grant money at U of M just because I worked in the financial aid division? That was Him.

Or when a lawyer, bored in line, offered to look over my legal filing and helped me get through the process? No lie—that was Him too.

Or the time I woke up as a teen coughing and managed to get everyone out of the house before the carbon monoxide kept us sleeping? Definitely Him.

Let's not forget the childhood asthma or the car accident that left the back seat in the front but somehow, I walked away.

If I had 10,000 tongues, I couldn't thank Him enough because I NEVER would have made it without HIM!

Your SHORT NEVER Would Have Made It list:

On My Own

How many times have you been on your own and made it through just fine?

Sometimes, it's absolutely wonderful to share experiences with someone else—dating, dinner, movies—those are all great to enjoy with a partner. But if you don't have someone to share them with, does that mean you shouldn't enjoy them at all? Even when life throws you a curveball, you can still embrace and enjoy life! I say this as someone who has been twice divorced and is now happily married for the third time.

Please know this:

 I dated myself, enjoyed myself, and loved me when I was on my own.

You can do it too! You've done it before. Just take a moment and think back. You've got this!

1. Birth
2. Driver's Tests / School Exams
3. Reading a book
4. Learning / Practicing an instrument
5. Treating yourself/ Spa / Shopping
6. Loving yourself / Self Care
7. Protecting your peace / Distancing you from drama
8. Breathing (without aid)
9. Sleeping peacefully (without aid)
10. Dying / Death

HOW MANY TIMES HAVE YOU MADE IT , JUST FINE, ON YOUR OWN?

POISON

DO YOU WILLINGLY EAT, DRINK, OR TAKE POISON? INQUIRING MINDS WANT TO KNOW. DO YOU SIT AROUND SIPPING BLEACH, NAIL POLISH, DETERGENT—OR MUD, EVEN? NO?

THEN WHY DO YOU KNOWINGLY ALLOW OTHER POISONS INTO YOUR MIND, BODY, AND SOUL?

IF YOU KNOW YOU'RE ALLERGIC TO NUTS, WHY ARE YOU EATING TRAIL MIX? IF YOU HAVE A FISH, SEAFOOD, OR SHELLFISH ALLERGY, WHY ARE YOU DIVING INTO A SEAFOOD BOIL WITH NO BENADRYL OR EPIPEN IN SIGHT?

AND LET'S TALK ABOUT RELATIONSHIPS. IF YOU KNOW SOMEONE DOESN'T LIKE YOU, WHY ARE YOU STILL TRYING TO BE NICE TO THEM, ENGAGING IN CONVERSATIONS, OR GIVING COMPLIMENTS? FOR WHATEVER REASON, THEY DON'T LIKE YOU. LET IT GO. SURE, YOU CAN TRY TO WORK THINGS OUT, BUT IF YOU'VE TRIED TIME AND AGAIN AND NOTHING CHANGES, IT'S TIME TO *PUSH—PRAY* UNTIL SOMETHING HAPPENS—AND STOP EXPOSING YOURSELF TO THE POISON. HERE'S THE TAKEAWAY: **TREAT YOURSELF, DON'T CHEAT YOURSELF. BE GOOD TO YOU!**

WWW.MRS1HEALTHYYOU.COM

SAFE LABELING

NON TOXIC THINGS/PEOPLE   **TOXIC THINGS/PEOPLE**

A GUIDELINE FOR THE HEALTHIEST YOU

21 Questions

How many times in life have you not asked a question and regretted it later? A lot? Yep, I know, me too.

Not anymore! I ask nicely, but I ask. Before Damon and I married, I asked him some **HARD** questions. Can I see your tax return and check stubs? What's your credit score? What's your health status? I told him I needed to see, have, and understand these reports before we could even think about getting engaged—and I was DEAD SERIOUS!

1 Healthy Y♥u

I'd made too many mistakes in life because I didn't ask enough questions, and this was NOT going to be another one. I loved him, YES, BUT I needed those questions answered to make an informed decision. I was a single mom, twice divorced, with jacked-up credit, and a few health issues. We would NOT be the new blind leading the blind.

I ASKED THE HARD QUESTIONS. Now, he could've said no, but he didn't, and we moved on. Nine years later, I'm thankful I asked and he answered.

FUTURE QUESTIONS

Family / Friends

Work

YOU

Purchases

Notes

RESPECT

When thinking of respect, there's a lot to consider.

I think the biggest piece of it is truly treating others how you want to be treated.

That means if you like to be listened to and valued in a conversation, you should, in turn, do the same when speaking with someone.
It means even if you disagree with someone, respecting their viewpoint and opinion.
It means, even when you're angry, being able to hold the conversation maturely, and not resorting to yelling or rudeness.
Ok, let's talk real talk.
I've been in situations where I felt my way was the only way and didn't care to even listen if the conversation differed from that.

Of course, this was with a very close friend or loved one.
So, when I saw them making a huge mistake, I wanted to jump in and stop them, right?
Well, in the past, I have.
Yelled, screamed, hung up, or stopped talking to them altogether.
All in hopes that they would see it my way or do what I though was best.
Now?

I listen and pray more. I sit back and wait to be asked, "What do you think?"
I take me out of the equation and allow that person/situation room to grow, learn, breathe, and mature.
This was part of my lesson and my reciprocation of respect.

This journey is both difficult and exciting all at the same time.
You see, if you've ever helped a toddler walk, it's kind of like that.
You're on edge, watching them take steps, fall, and maybe even hurt themselves.
But all you can do is stand by with guardrails of prayer!
Especially when you're talking about grown folks, living their lives, not asking for your opinion, not needing your money, just needing your respect.

Ooooh, it ain't easy! But their battle ain't yours!
Everybody's got their own battles and demons to fight.
Take care of your own house and wait on the sidelines out of respect, until you're tagged if needed.
Give them/the situation the same respect you want, and use that energy in another useful area.

RETROSPECT OF
RESPECT

PAST	FUTURE
In the past, I've messed up respect by:	*In the future respect can look like :*
○	○
○	○
○	○
○	○
○	○

REFLECTION
OF RESPECT

To Amazing

If you're reading this, how *amazing* is your life?
And if you're a little older, how amazing was your life?
I think of my grandma. She often tells me, "Have a good time, while you can!"
At 97 years young, she has done, seen, enjoyed, and experienced a lot!

There's not much we can do about trials, tribulations, genetic health issues, death, and moments of sorrow.
BUT you can choose to make the portions of your life that you can control truly amazing!

You can handle trials and tribulations with grace.
You can be proactive with your health.
And you can choose to make the rest of your life amazing despite the moments of sorrow that arise.

I've had moments I'm glad are behind me and times I'm embarrassed to even look back on.
But what I can control? I make as amazing as possible.

Am I proud of two failed marriages? No.
But the marriage I have now? SO AMAZING!

WHAT'S AMAZING ALREADY?

_____

_____

_____

_____

_____

_____

WHAT CAN BE MORE AMAZING?

_____

_____

_____

_____

_____

_____

Time after Time

The definition of insanity is doing the same thing over and over again and expecting different results. (I didn't even have to fully type this; the computer completed the statement for me because it knows it!)

What's my point?
Time waits for no one and is promised to no one! So, why keep making the same mistakes when time is of the essence?

Ok, let's talk. In my past, I made some mistakes. One evident area? My choice in men. I used to have a type—tall, dark, and chocolate! I even found my first and second husbands that way.

Now, don't get me wrong; I learned, matured, and gained something valuable from both relationships. (I got my beautiful daughters from my first marriage.)

But when it came to husband #3? *He chose me.* He looked for me!
Although I saw him first, I sat my Type A, aggressive, go-getter self down and let him find me.

Proverbs 18:22 (NIV) says, *"He who finds a wife finds what is good and receives favor from the Lord."*

Nine years later, I'm so thankful I did something different—and got a better result.

Here's the takeaway:
Every case is different, but quit wasting your time doing the same thing over and over again. Time is precious. Make the change, and watch the difference.

TRACKS OF TIME

DATE :   /   /

PAST

FUTURE

In the past, I've wasted time by:

In the future better uses of my time look like :

- ○
- ○
- ○
- ○
- ○

- ○
- ○
- ○
- ○
- ○

REFLECTING ON MY TIME

HOW BIG IS YOUR UMBRELLA? WHO'S UNDER IT?
HOW LONG THEY BEEN UNDER IT?
ARE YOU WET?

I am a protector! My sister's keeper! A mama bear! A lioness! I am all of those women. But you know what? I've learned to take care of me, too.

I can't get sick from a cold because I gave you my umbrella and got soaked myself. No more.

I can't be more concerned about your bad situation than you are. No more.

I can't do more research than you to help fix your problem while you're busy doing something else that won't help your situation. No more.

Here's the thing: I am always here for those who genuinely need me and are willing to work with me to resolve their issues. If that's you? I've got you! People have been there for me, and I am eternally grateful for their support.

But let me be clear—I will always support, never enable.

Note: You can SHARE your umbrella NOT give it to somebody then get sick! NO MORE!!!

SUPPORT

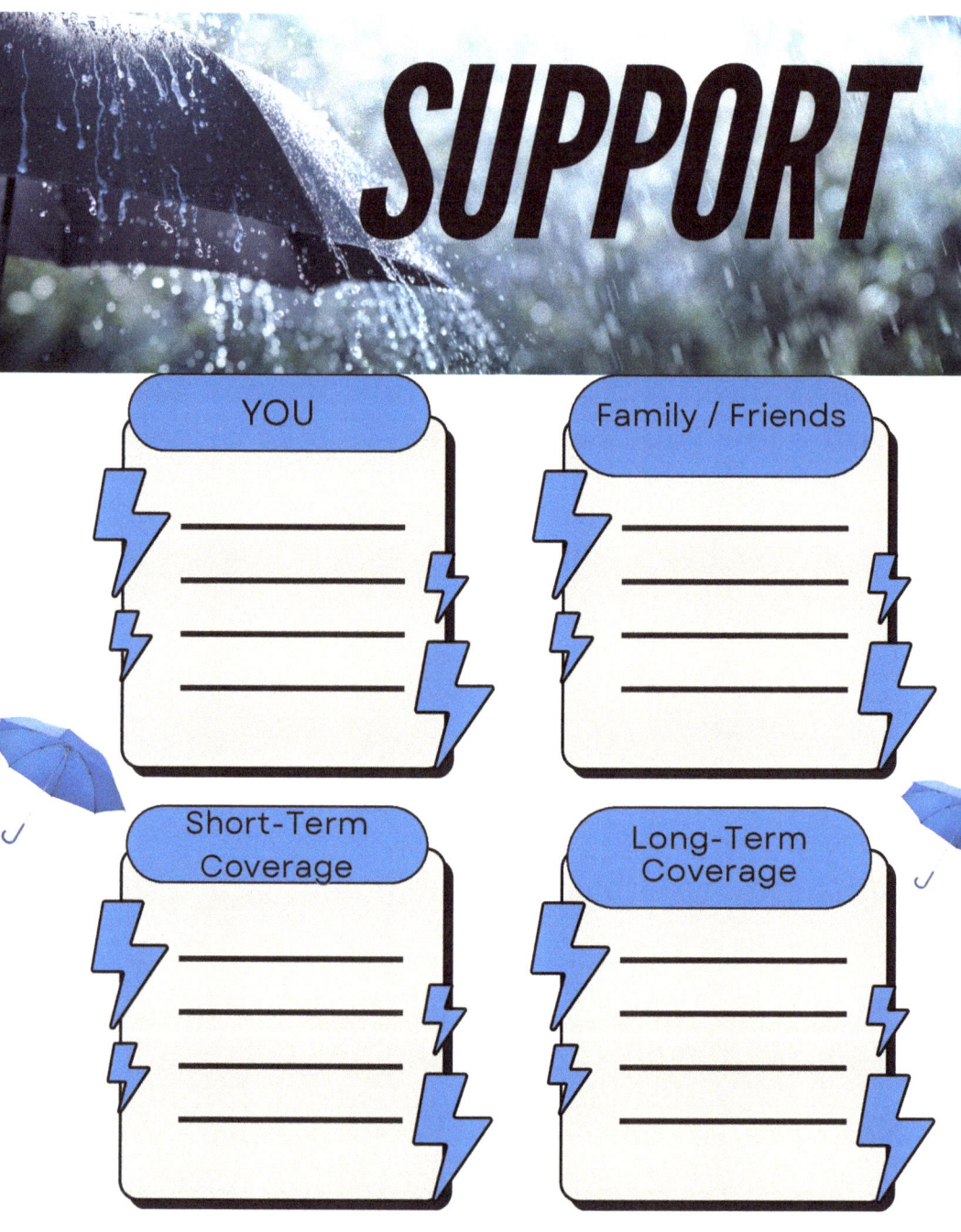

YOU

Family / Friends

Short-Term Coverage

Long-Term Coverage

Note: Don't get swept up in a tsunami for temporary folk.

Vogue

Vogue: noun

1. **the prevailing fashion or style at a particular time:**

Hopefully, you're changing and growing gracefully. Think about the afros and bell bottoms of the '70s, the USED and DAMAGED style of the '90s! Remember Starter jackets? Yes, I wanted a sheepskin coat! I sure did! Or how about a scooter? An Elite or Spree? Now, a scooter may work in certain countries or cities. It might even be ideal for certain age groups or occupations, but it's not my choice today. Being a Midwestern dweller, the ice and snow don't mix well with a scooter for me. I'll stick with driving cars, thank you.

Bottom line: I do what's best for me right now. Today, as an empty nester, I enjoy wearing tasteful clothing that shows off my weight loss, living life in peace and comfort, traveling, and showing love.

At this stage in my life, I'm going to vogue to the music that makes me feel good, while wearing what makes me look good.

1 HEALTHY Y♥U

Today's fashion/style of life: Date: _____

_____
_____
_____
_____
_____
_____
_____
_____
_____
_____
_____
_____
_____
_____
_____
_____
_____
_____
_____

What's Love Got to Do With It?

For me, love is everything. Yes, I'm definitely a romantic—but not hopelessly so! I am a strong, independent sista, and for the most part, I can handle things on my own. But I choose and prefer not to do it alone. That said, I will not settle for just anyone simply to have someone by my side. I won't redate or remarry (in my case) just to have a plus one.

I LOVE my husband, and I'm so thankful for him, BUT I also LOVE ME enough—enough to make sure he was the best choice for me. He complements me, supports me, and brings an almost effortless presence to my life and family.

For me, it wasn't about money, provision, property, or assets; those weren't the priorities. It was about what God wanted for me. My choice was him, and he chose me.

After doing things my way for so long, I finally let my love for Christ guide me to the love of my life.

Now, everyone has free will. You can choose who you want, how you want, when you want. Just don't cheat yourself! Everything that's good **TO YOU** ain't good **FOR YOU**! I've learned some lessons the hard way. Now I really try to listen more and lean **NOT** to **MY** own understanding. It may take time but if you "Wait for Love" it will be worth it.

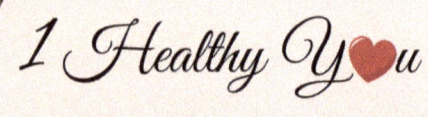

Today's feelings of/for love: *Date:* _____

_____
_____
_____
_____
_____
_____
_____
_____
_____
_____
_____
_____
_____
_____
_____
_____
_____
_____
_____

Follow your heart and don't give up!
Be happy in the meantime in between time.
When you reach your goal/love, enjoy and share the love.

Sealed with a kiss.
French Kiss
Kiss and make up
Kiss and make it better
Kiss my grits!

Kisses can mean different things to different people. For me, they're special and almost sacred. That's why I always say, "Don't be kissing babies on their mouths!" "Don't let everybody kiss on that baby!" and "Don't let everybody kiss you!"
A kiss is sweet, meaningful, and not something to hand out like Halloween candy to anyone who comes to your door. Think about it—do you want to treat yourself to something meaningful, or waste time on a trick? Stop giving precious moments to temporary people. Protect what's special.
1 Healthy You

XO

Thoughts/
Changes/
Reflections :

_____
_____
_____
_____
_____
_____
_____

_____
_____
_____
_____
_____
_____
_____
_____
_____
_____

1 HEALTHY Y♥U

Yes

Yes, Lord! Yes to Your will and Your way! Even though I don't always move as You want me to, my answer to You is always YES! Without hesitation or question, it's YES because I trust You completely—I know You'll never lead me wrong.

Outside of God? For me, no one gets an automatic "YES" every time—not even the Grands or Grandma. I aim to make the best decision for myself and for others in every situation.

For instance, even though my little Ace might want to eat five candy bars a day, the answer is no. Why? Because everything that's good to you isn't always good for you!

Take a job making six figures—it sounds good, right? But if you're never home, stressed at work, can't enjoy your earnings, and hate what you do, the answer to staying in that role might need to be NO. Instead, saying YES to a different opportunity could align better with your overall happiness and purpose.

As we grow older, the decisions we make have to work for us in the short and long term—financially, emotionally, spiritually, and physically. Every choice should be measured by asking, Should the answer really be YES? Do YOU. Be the BEST you. And always stay TRUE to you!

Yes

WHO/WHAT IS YOUR YES TO?

_____

_____

_____

_____

_____

_____

_____

_____

_____

_____

_____

Zillionaire

Dreaming is essential for growth, I believe.
"If you dream it, you can achieve it." – Zig Ziglar
In my dreams, I'm the director. I get to choose the
cast, decide the storyline, and call "end scene"
whenever I want. I can wake up, dream again, and
rewrite the entire movie if I choose.

The real question is, *What are you dreaming of and
why*? Is it always about money because you grew
up poor? Or about love because you never felt
any?

For me? Sure, I want financial stability. I also
deeply value being in a happy marriage. I find joy
in helping and blessing others. I treasure being
healthy and happy in every sense—mentally,
emotionally, and physically. And I don't take
mental stability for granted.

I dream of becoming the healthiest, most complete
version of myself and leaving that legacy for my
family and my community.

Yes, I want to be financially comfortable—at the
very least—but I also want to be rich in
knowledge, spirit, Spirit, and health.

Absolutely! I want to be a zillionaire in both
wealth and health!
1 Healthy You

Zillionaire Vision

(Day): _____ (Month): _____ (Year): _____

(Remember/Think/Dream)

WHAT kind of zillionaire do you want to be? How will you get there?

WHAT steps do you need to begin to get there?

HEALTH

TRAVEL

CAREER

FINANCES

RELATIONSHIPS

SPIRITUALITY

Mrs. 1 Healthy You

Alana Nicole

Alana Dillard is a proud native of Detroit with a deep love for her city! She currently serves as an Attendance Agent within the Detroit Public Schools Community District. With over 15 years of experience in education, Alana has made a lasting impact in her field.

Although working in education wasn't her childhood dream, it has become her adult passion and purposeful calling. Alana's journey into education may have started by chance, but her love for it was immediate and unwavering. Those who know her best often say, "She's always trying to teach or tell somebody something!" For them, her career in education feels like a natural fit.

Alana Dillard is happily married and the proud mother of three adult children. She also embraces her role as "Gigi" to one granddaughter, one grandson, and five bonus grandchildren.

Academically accomplished, Alana holds a Bachelor of Science in Business Management, a Master of Business Administration/Public Administration, and a Master of Arts in Education/Adult Education and Training.

Through her non-profit organization, 1Healthy You, Alana shares her knowledge, care, and goodwill with as many people in the community as possible. Since its founding in 2021, 1Healthy You has been a platform for Alana's passion to help, educate, and empower others beyond her chosen career in education.

The organization is dedicated to helping individuals reduce stress levels and prevent heart disease by providing essential resources, information, and services to improve their daily lives. Alana frequently volunteers through 1Healthy You, showing people how to become the healthiest versions of themselves.

As Alana herself proudly states, "I am Mrs. 1Healthy You."

This is her first book, a testament to her mission of spreading knowledge and inspiration for a healthier, more fulfilling life.

I _pray_ you enjoyed it!

What did you think?

Did you know **every** song?

When you didn't know the song, did you look it up?

Did you **dance** in your spot while thinking of the lyrics?

Did you learn something new?

Did this _help_ you?

I have so many questions, but the biggest one is just _how_ _much_ did you like it?

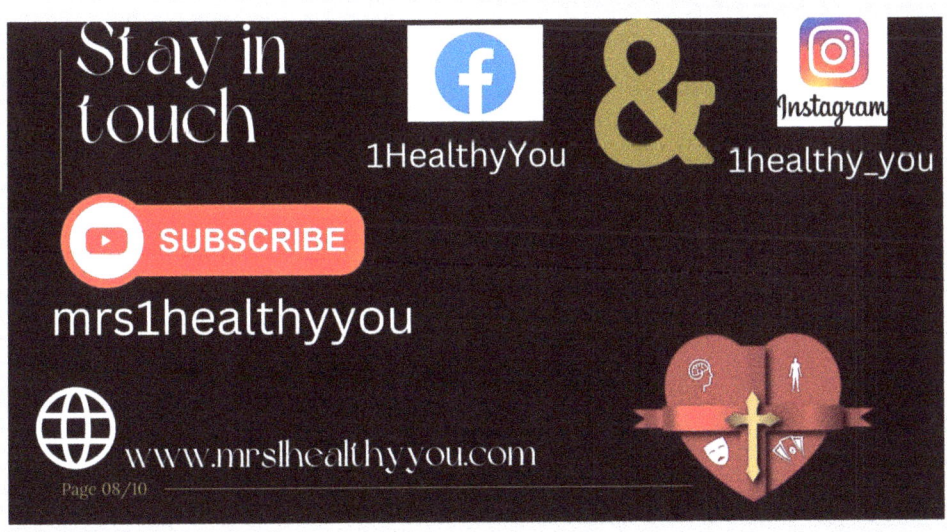

ACKNOWLEDGEMENTS

First and foremost, giving honor to God, who IS the head of my life—I thank You! I thank You for this vision and these words. Without You, I am nothing, and this work would not exist.

I thank You for EVERYTHING!

To my husband, Damon Dillard Sr.: Thank you for loving me and supporting me through everything! The third time truly was the charm, baby, and that's exactly what you are! I love you, honey.

To my children and GRANDS: Arricka, Amaya, Ambre', and ACE—thank you. You all are such a big part of my rhythm and melody. I'm grateful for the good times, the tough moments, and the love we share. I love you all!

To my fathers, Phillip Rolack I and Craig Anderson Sr., and my matriarch, Birdie Jarmon: thank you! You have given me life, support, love, encouragement, and lessons I can never repay. Y'all created this monster (lol), and I'm so glad you did! I love you!

THANK YOU

Last but never least, to my cherished family members and friends—thank you from the bottom of my heart. You are always in my heart and never forgotten! (PLUS, here's your personal shout-out AND another reason to grab TWO books: one to keep and one to share!)

Listed below, in no particular order, are my living angels. I hope you love it as much as I do!
Godma Hellen Paceley, Auntie Shirley Clanton, Auntie Deborah Robertson, Auntie Deidra Jarmon-Miller, Chappelle Brown, Phillip Rolack II, Kamela Diaz, Raikia Perry, Auntie Patricia Moncrease, Auntie Jackie Buchannan, Auntie Lovica Gilmore, Jeannaka Andrews, Melissa Hill, LaTonia Walker, AP Terri Draper, Cousin Charles Thomas, 1HY, Deidre Hunt, Sherita Brown, British Burnett, Tasha Smith, The Ladies League of Detroit, Auntie Deborah Payne, Sistar Jenice Hand, Ms. Sandra Harris, Sharon Harris, Sedrick Cashaw, Cousin Deshawn Williams, Doris Rue, Robin Parker-Grant, my sister-in-love Carmen Fahey, my godsister La Toi Smith, my godbrother Lamar Hightower, Sedrick Cashaw, my bonus son Damon Dillard Jr., and my bonus grands: Nevaeh, Malachi, Izaiah, Journey, and Kyrie Dillard.
To my nieces, nephews, cousins, aunts, uncles, and dear friends—if you're reading this and your name isn't listed, please charge it to my head and not my heart!
To ALL my village and supporters, thank you endlessly. Your love and encouragement mean the world to me! ♥

I PRAY YOU ENJOYED MY BOOK AND ALL THE LESSONS
I'VE SHARED WITH YOU.
THE MUSIC? A LIL BONUS FROM ME TO YOU.

LOVE, ALANA NICOLE
AKA
MRS 1 HEALTHY YOU

www.ingramcontent.com/pod-product-compliance
Lightning Source LLC
Chambersburg PA
CBHW051552120626
46551CB00013B/1482